STILL STRONG

The Short Story of Dian

Anthony Teens

Table of Content

Chapter 1

Dian, 17yrs old girl grew up and lived with her parents and siblings who came from the western part of Africa.

Dian who is the second child in the house met a good life and a happy family when she was 2 she was enrolled in a nursery school together with her elder sister Deborah, who look just like her, as the only child Katherine had then she made certain she gave them quality education and more even when she wasn't working.

Nathan, the husband who was a graduate and working-class,

showered all his love and money on them as the only family he had, and things went well.

Katherine decided to have a maid since the house responsibility became too much for her, she took in a daughter of a close family friend Evelyn.

Though Evelyn was not just the daughter of a family friend but the second daughter to Nathan's elder brother.

Deborah was 3 while Dian was 2 when both of them were sexually abused by Evelyn and were threatened not to say a word to their parent as time went on.

Dian was 4 and Deborah 5 when Evelyn became pregnant in their house and accused Nathan to be responsible for it, the story became confusing but the truth came out that the pregnancy belongs to an unknown street boy who had claimed to be in love with Evelyn.

Nathan, on the other hand, changed totally, he became less concerned about the children, at this time Katherine had taken in her third child Mandy.

This is when every effort she made in getting a job came forth and Mandy became the only child who looked different.

Katherine was employed in a bank to work as a cleaner which made her very happy that should be able to help her husband with some house responsibilities.

Mandy was 2 and everything was perfect, Deborah and Dian were enrolled in a public primary with the effort of their mother as Nathan showed no concern because he was disappointed and needed a male child, Mandy at this time was also enrolled in the same primary school with Debby and Dian to start with the lower children of her age.

Things became tough as Nathan started drinking and smoking, was picked up by police several times, and was released from jail with the help of Katherine.

At this point, Katherine tried advising him to stop drinking, and smoking and focus, he stopped smoking only but continued drinking.

Chapter 2

When Deborah and Dian were in secondary school still with the help of their mother this time Nathan their father had lost his job and started a rafter business which he didn't succeed due to his drinking attitude, was arrested by militants, misplaced the rafter engine to an unknown person not to talk of the lending of money from people which Katherine end up paying back with interest, this time Katherine had already given birth to her fourth child Bridget and took in her 5th child.

Nathan's attitude keeps going on and on because of the excuse of all four children are females. Katherine became the father and mother of the house since Nathan showed no interest in sending the kids to school or providing money for feeding, he believed that female Education is not important and useful.

Katherine put to birth a boy and Nathan was very happy, the birth of the baby called for a celebration.

At 8 months Fred started school because Katherine's maternity leave had expired, Nathan needed a male child he had but yet still didn't care much about him.

Katherine took up the responsibility of taking care of all her 5 children by herself alone since she wasn't loved by her family, she made sure that her children never go to bed hungry, and things became very hard as she is the breadwinner of the house.

Fred became sick and was taken to the hospital for treatment at 1 year, Dian wasn't done with her secondary together with Deborah, and it was time for Dian to write her upper grade 3 exams, barely 2 days before the exams Katherine lost Fred to sickle cell disease through Katherine doesn't believe cus there is no trace of such disease in her family.

Dian was heartbroken cus that was their only brother and the only person she was close to, Katherine couldn't bear the pain of losing her only son, her happiness.

Time went fast and Deborah was done with secondary school, it was a holiday and Katherine decided to spend it in her homeland with the kids, at this time Dian had already dropped out of school since her mother couldn't further her and her dad Nathan wasn't interested.

During the holiday at the village where Katherine comes from, it was there Dian was raped by her uncle.

Dian was sad and depressed, she regretted ever knowing and calling him uncle, at that time she was just 15 years old. she lived her life with that scarce in her heart, she thought of ways to tell her mother which she finally did, and she tried her best to let go of the past and live in her future, things went well though still hard, Dian was given out to stay with a pastor and render help, her new family seems to be nice to her, at this time her own family couldn't afford to pay for the rent of a house again and was disgraced by the house owner ago threw their things outside.

Katherine had no choice since she didn't have enough to pay for a house, so she decided to live in the church till she is financially balanced, at this point she had already taken in and birth to a baby girl Elena, though she expected a but still gave her the motherly love she deserves, at 1 Elena became strong and beautiful, things looked as if it was going right but something was still wrong.

Katherine tried her best to avoid another pregnancy since she was the only person catering to the family, but she couldn't, so she took in the pregnancy of her 6th child.

She felt bad and was helpless. She thought of what to do and decided to keep the baby even with all the embarrassment she received.

She held onto the fact that every child is from God whether by mistake or not, whether by wedlock or not.

Elena was just 2 when Katherine brought forth the 6th child and lo and behold it was a baby boy after all the prayers, fasting, and sleepless night, God answered, and

Pharez coming into the world brought happiness and joy.

Chapter 3

One week after Katherine was delivered she died due to bleeding after childbirth leaving the baby just one week old, all this happened when Deborah had traveled out a year before Mandy was 11, and Bridget was 9. Elena 2 and Dian 16.

Dian as the only elderly person took up the responsibility of watching over her siblings with the help of Katherine's colleagues since her father Nathan was not doing anything, before Katherine's death, Dian was about writing her final exams in a secondary school which she couldn't complete because of the sudden dismiss of her mother but was able to pay someone to write for her through the help of a man she met while working.

After one month, Dian and her siblings were picked up by their uncle to accommodate and feed them. Dian was happy at least someone had finally remembered them not knowing that it was getting to the worst point.

At 16 Dian had so many suitors who came, some with the intention of marriage, the married men also came intending to make her their side chick, she lived her life following what she has heard and understanding what she has been through.

The thought of all the things her mother Katherine told her, how she grew up in a family where there is no love, no one cares since her marriage with Nathan was against her mother's will, and all the curses her mother later upon her, if not for the mighty hands of God she would've committed suicide long ago but she still gave them that love they deserve.

It came into Dian's barely 3 days after Katherine passed out, her mother Gladys died, it looked as if they planned it, all this thought mind as she vowed never to make the mistake her mother made which cost her her life, Katherine never listened to the advice of not letting your husband over control you.

The thought of furthering herself into the university came to her mind, she wants to read

Mechanical engineering and has no support since the father she had was just like not having a father.

Pharez was dedicated and Katherine was buried, things looked as if they will change while in Jeremy's house the uncle did not until a few months of their stay there Jeremy's wife Angela became tired of accommodating them since she was the breadwinner of the house and had also accommodated some of her siblings and their children.

Looking at the way things were Dian decided to work to help herself and her siblings, her effort to look for work was successful, she was employed in a school as a cleaner and she was very happy and diligent, punctual, and respectful.

Chapter 4

Time went very fast and the school opened another branch on 5th avenue in New York, America close to the world trade center and she was among the people transferred to that side, it was like a dream come true for Dian since she has always wanted to be outside the country, she was also at the same time given promotion to be an assistant teacher and was paid well.

She used that opportunity and bought the American University entrance exams form which passed with flying colors and was given admission to study Mechanical engineering at New York University, the country's university.

She rented her house and brought her siblings to stay with her including Deborah, she resigned from work since she could no longer manage to go to work daily and schooling.

A few weeks after she resigned, she was called to the Blue house to work with the Education team, she accepted the appointment and gave them her condition, Deborah on the other hand owned the biggest fashion designing company in New York PROUD, and also a well-known journalist and TV presenter, they brought their dad Nathan to stay with them since no matter what happens he's still the father.

Deborah was engaged to one of the youngest business owners and the CEO of GREEN HOTELS, one of the biggest and most well-known hotels in Dallas Texas, America.

Dian remembered being told that every situation of life is a ride and she concluded that she is enjoying this ride, Dian traveled to almost all the countries in the world as a part of learning and she became one of the wells know big engineers all over the world, Nathan regretted ever saying that female children are not useful and their education is not important.

Remembering where she started from and where she is today tears rolled down her cheeks as she wished her mother Katherine was still alive to see her effort and her strength, at the same time she smiled at herself for being strong and not giving up.

TO GOD BE THE GLORY.

www.ingramcontent.com/pod-product-compliance
Lightning Source LLC
LaVergne TN
LVHW010515160826
845677LV00012B/2864

* 9 7 9 8 3 5 8 9 9 3 3 8 9 *